What happens when you're Generous?

Tommy "Urban D." Kyllonen

Tranzlation Leadership
TAMPA, FLORIDA

Tranzlation Leadership
1235 E. Fowler Ave. Tampa, Florida 33612
© 2020 by Tommy Kyllonen

All rights reserved. No part of this book may be reproduced in any form without written permission from Tranzlation Leadership.

Unless otherwise indicated, all scripture quotations are taken from the Holy Bible, New Living Translation, copyright © 1996, 2004, 2015 by Tyndale House Foundation. Used by permission of Tyndale House Publishers, Inc. Carol Stream, Illinois 60188. All rights reserved.

While any stories in this book are true, some names and identifying information may have been changed to protect the privacy of individuals.

Cover + Interior Design: Edward "Spec" Bayonet | iAMbayo.net
Photography: Abigail Medina and Crossover's Social Media Team

ISBN: 978-1-7327782-6-9 (print)

ISBN: 978-1-7327782-7-6 (ebook)

This book is also available in digital and audio formats

Printed in the United States

www.urband.org

*100% of the proceeds of this book are donated to
Crossover Church and Love Our City.*

Table of Contents

pg.08 Introduction

pg.10 Chapter 1: It changes your Heart.

pg.28 Chapter 2: It changes your Situation.

pg.42 Chapter 3: It changes your Church.

pg.52 Chapter 4: It changes your City.

pg.70 Epilogue

INTRODUCTION

Thank You.
Gracias.
Merci.
Grazi.
Domo Arigato.
Do Jeh, Daw-Dyeh.

You may have received this book as a gift because you recently gave to a church or an organization. Thank you for your giving. You may have purchased this book as you were curious about generosity and philanthropy. Either way I'm grateful your heart is leaning towards learning more about giving back.

Giving is a big deal. Some of you recently gave for the very first time, while others may give on a regular basis. Some of you give without thinking much about it, while others wrestle with the financial sacrifice it may require of your family. Either way, giving is significant and it can make a huge difference in our world.

My prayer is that this book will open up your eyes to what really begins to happen when you're generous. If you do it intentionally it can change you and many things around you. Giving has changed me and my family in so many ways. This short book will share some Biblical principles and real life stories about generosity and the change it develops from the inside out.

CHAPTER 1

It changes your Heart.

Generosity all starts with your heart. ***"God doesn't want your money"***, he wants your heart. God radically changed my heart while I was in college. Previously, I was a pretty selfish guy. I thought only about myself, my money and my possessions. When I started a solid relationship with Jesus my heart began to shift. I became more generous in several new ways. I volunteered countless hours of ministry during my college years at local churches and through a Hip-Hop Ministry that I started. My heart was continuing to transform to become more like Jesus. My generosity grew with my time, talent and treasure. My goals were no longer about me balling out, but now it was about being in the center of God's will. I was ready to go wherever he called me. I realized what an exciting adventure life could be when I trusted God with everything. When my wife and I first got married we were broke. I had just finished college and was starting my first job as the very first youth pastor at Crossover Church in Tampa, Florida. I had a big salary package of $100 a month. Then a business man from the church jumped in and said, "I'll give an additional $500 a month if you come." I knew this is where God wanted me, so I came on faith. I was ready to work another part time job to make ends meet. My heart was at the church. I was willing to be generous with my time. Whenever we are generous, the scripture also says God will provide so we can continue to be even more generous.

After I accepted the position at Crossover I watched God continue to move. The summer before coming to Crossover I had completed an internship at a church in Clearwater, Florida. A month after I accepted the position at Crossover they generously started supporting me as an urban missionary for the first year. That filled in most of the gaps for me to be almost full-time at the church. Again, I was ready to go and get a part time job working at least one night a week waiting tables. My heart was in the right place and God again continued to move. My pastor Joe McCutchen encouraged me to record an album. I was so naive about the music industry I replied back to my pastor, "But, I'm not signed to a record label, you have to be signed to make an album." I had no idea. He quickly schooled me that I could make an album independently by renting studio time and pressing up the physical copies myself (this was before digital music). He challenged me and said, "Your heart is in ministry and you are a good rapper, so why go and work at a restaurant one night a week? Instead, you can go out and minister at other churches a couple nights a month doing ministry and music and do something you love. At the same time this will help provide for your family." A light bulb went on! My heart was in the right place, but I still had no idea how I was going to get beats and production for the album. Again I watched God provide. A few weeks later I met Marty White and Johnny Jamz who saw my heart and generously volunteered to help me make my first independent album. They donated their home studio and their talent to produce the music. Five months later the album was done and God quickly opened up several opportunities for me to go out and minister through my music, testimony and preaching.

For many years my music ministry supported my family and helped me continue to serve at Crossover Church in a full-time capacity, even though my pay from the church was part-time or in some seasons non-existent when the outside support stopped. To many people it might sound crazy to work full-time for a small part-time salary and some weeks and months even work for free. But, my heart had changed and this was a way I could be generous. The amazing thing is we always watched God provide and supply all of our needs. The details of my story will look different than yours, but as your heart becomes more like him your generosity will grow and you'll watch God do miracles.

My corny treasure.

Before you get tempted to think you can't relate because you don't work at a church or because you've made lots of mistakes, let me be honest and tell you that there were moments when I missed it. There were seasons that my heart got distracted.

*"I'm human.
I make mistakes just like you".*

If we're not careful we can chase treasure and Jesus made it clear in Matthew 6:21 where He said, "Wherever your treasure is, there the desires of your heart will also be." After I first got married we were using our wedding money to pay off some debt. My father had some recent investments in the stock market that paid off really well. He actually doubled his money in thirty days two different times. It was in a risky stock option called "futures". My dad had made thousands of dollars in the past few months, so I was willing to give it a try. He connected me with his stock broker and he blessed me with $1,000 and I put in $1,000 from our wedding money. Back then $1,000 was like $10,000, so my wife was super hesitant. But, I was blindly confident that this could work.

    I had a plan for God. You ever had a plan for God? How did that work out for you? My plan was that this could be a stream of income that we'd use pay off all of our debt and also be able to fund us to continue in urban ministry. Sounded nice, right? I thought my heart was in the right place, so God would bless it, but this wasn't God's plan. But, I wasn't really listening, so I put my money into this corn stock. Before that, I knew nothing and cared nothing about corn. But, now that some of my treasure was there, so some of my heart shifted there. I was reading articles about corn and the upcoming forecast. I learned how to read the stocks in the newspaper and check everyday how the corn stock was doing. I thought about it. I day dreamed about it. I even prayed about it... "God bless the corn!" Well, I watched my stock start growing. My $2,000 soon grew to $2,500 and then $3,000. It went up to $3,200 at one point and I was partying! But, then it started to slide back. I called my stockbroker and he told me not to worry about it, this happens. Soon it even slid below the $2,000 I had put in. Oh yeah, by the way... you can lose what you put in. It dropped to half of what I put in and my stock guy kept telling me to hold on, it was going to bounce back. My heart was heavy. I was worried. Why? Because some of my treasure was planted... in the corn. A few months later I realized what a corny deal it was. I had lost every single dollar! It was all gone. I was crushed. I asked God for forgiveness as I realized my heart had got distracted in something that wasn't his plan for me.

    It's really difficult to get our hearts to consistently become more like God's in the area of generosity. We live in a culture where there are so many unhealthy dynamics around money and possessions. It's defined as a consumer culture. It's in the air we breathe. It makes it really hard to be content. Everywhere we look there is always the new upgraded version of everything coming out. Consumerism can be defined as "our desire to acquire more for ourselves when we already have enough." We already have 20 pairs of shoes, but we want another one. Have you ever saved up for something that you really wanted and thought, "When I get it, I will be totally satisfied. This is the last thing I need… really!" Then you purchased it and you quickly realized, "I've been duped." You may have been temporarily excited, but it didn't bring you the permanent satisfaction you had hoped for. Finding contentment in consumerism will always be elusive. Many of us may work really hard to change our habits. We get more disciplined, work on self-control and stay away from the mall. But, before you change your habits, you need to change your heart. A better relationship with money starts with the heart. Altering how you think and feel is the only way to bring a lasting difference in how you act.

Jesus wants your Heart.

"I'm a natural born taker. Don't judge. So are you!"

It's in our nature. But, God's nature is generous. He is a giver. He wants us to become more like him. Jesus knows our hearts are deeply connected to our money and our possessions. In the Bible he told stories called parables. 16 out of the 38 parables he told were about money and possessions. Jesus talked more about money and the handling of it than he talked about heaven, hell, prayer or faith. God wants our heartbeat to be in rhythm with his in every area. He knows what a big deal our money and our stuff can be. If this area is not aligned and in sync with God's heart, our lives can quickly fall outside his plan.

Money and possessions are personal. We spend so much time, effort and energy trying to make it, spend it, save it, invest it and hopefully give it. It can define us. The way we handle it defines our character. In Matthew 6:24 Jesus said, "No one can serve two masters. Either you will hate the one and love the other, or you will be devoted to the one and despise the other. You cannot serve both God and money." If we don't handle money properly it can end up being our master. If we don't have the proper perspective on money it can also end up being our master. You may have heard that the Bible says money is the root of all evil. I heard that before too, but that is absolutely incorrect. It's taken out of context from 1 Timothy 6:10. This is how it reads, "The LOVE of money is the root of all kinds of evil."

"It's not money itself, but it's the love of it. If I love money, it will lead me. But, if I can learn to lead money, it will serve me."

How do I lead money? We have to be in rhythm with the heart of Jesus. We have to come to the understanding that God owns it all and we are just managers. Yes, we may own some things, but God helped us get everything we have, and technically we only get to have these things temporarily. I've never seen a U-haul connected to a hearse. We can't take any of this stuff with us. The Pharoah's of Egypt tried and that didn't work out so well. When we grasp this reality we have the opportunity to lead money and have it serve us. Ultimately, it's not serving us, it's serving God's purposes because we're in rhythm with him. We want our lives to bring him shine.

There is a battle going on for our hearts. One of the biggest areas the war rages is with our money and our stuff. The enemy knows that if he can get us messed up with money, he can get us off track. This is a huge struggle point for Americans. In Tampa we have a lot of traffic as our city is growing so quickly. There are two major highways that intersect in downtown and it is notoriously known as "Malfunction Junction". It's been under construction multiple times and they are about to do another major expansion in the next few years again. It seems that everywhere you look around our city there is road construction. Road construction is annoying as it slows us down. Satan is in the business of creating road construction in our lives. He comes right next to the track we are on and starts to attack us in several different areas. He puts up some barricades tries to get us to take a detour and jump from God's track onto his track. He uses the pride detour where he gets us to buy into the idea that we are better than others, or we deserve more. He uses the ownership detour where he convinces us that we earned it, we built it, we worked hard for it, it's ours and we don't need to share anything with anyone. He uses the materialism detour where we know we can't afford it, but when we go down this track we'll do anything to get it. We'll borrow money we don't have (credit cards), or maybe even cheat, steal or manipulate to get what we want. Beware of the detours and quick exits that can take you off God's track. It may seem like it's a quicker route to get where you want to be, but it always ends up putting you behind even further.

> *"How much is enough? Just a little bit more"* - John Rockefeller

How much is enough? This was a question that was asked to John Rockefeller who was America's first Billionaire in the early 1900's. His answer was "just a little bit more." If Rockefeller wanted a little more, what about you? How will you know when you have enough to make you happy? Research has shown that people that moved from lower income to higher income did not increase their happiness. Some really remarkable research was done between the world's richest and the world's poorest. The Forbes "400" list was given a survey and their satisfaction was rated at exactly the same level as the people of Masai of Kenya and the Intuit people in northern Greenland, who have no electricity or running water.

> *"If you are dependent on money, you will never have enough. If on the other hand, you are dependent on God, you will always have enough."* - Ron Blue

In 2008 I traveled to Africa and saw people living in extreme poverty in a shanty town in shacks made from wood and cardboard. It was humbling to see their living conditions, but the thing that stuck out was their happiness. They were smiling ear to ear and didn't ask us for anything. In fact, they offered us bottled waters and wanted to sit and talk and pray for us. There is a saying that says in America we have everything, so we worship God with nothing. In Africa they have nothing, so they worship God with everything. Sometimes the more we have can draw us farther away from God's heart and farther away from the contentment we long for. How do we find contentment? What is the secret? I love what Paul says in Philippians 4:11-13, "Not that I was ever in need, for I have learned how to be content with whatever I have. I know how to live on almost nothing or with everything. I have learned the secret of living in every situation, whether it is with a full stomach or empty, with plenty or little. For I can do everything through Christ, who gives me strength."

You're rich!

You are rich! Yes, I'm talking to you. You are absolutely, positively incredibly rich. Now, you might be thinking I'm talking about being spiritually rich because we are God's children and blah, blah, blah. No... I'm talking about cash money rich! Yes, that's you. Yes, that's me. That's us! Most Americans don't feel rich and we are!

> **"Most Americans think we are generous and we aren't! Ouch."**

Most of you reading this don't feel rich because there are others out there that are a lot richer than us and when we compare ourselves to them... we feel broke. But we are in a bubble. A rich bubble. Most of you have a car and if you do that puts you in the top 10% of people in the world. Most of you drove your cars this week and went to eat at a restaurant where someone took your order, cooked for you and cleaned up after you. Then you drove home and when some of you pulled up you pressed a button and you parked your car in it's own room. Cars have their own rooms in our country. But many people have so much extra stuff we fill our car's room and our car can't even fit in there. We walked into our house and it's climate controlled. We're rich! We have a bathroom in our house, many of us have 2 or 3 of them and when we press a button our stuff magically goes away, while many people around the world just have a hole. If you still don't believe me go to www.globalrichlist.com and you can type in your annual income and it will give you an estimate of where you are compared to the rest of the planet. Even if you are at America's poverty level for a family of four ($25,750) you are still in the top 2% of the world.

On a global scale we're very rich, but we're not very generous. The average American only gives away 2.8% of their income. You would think that richer people give more, but the opposite actually happens. For people that make more than $100,000 per year their giving average drops to 2.6% of their income. Many people have a desire to give more, but they feel that they can't. I grew up with a scarcity mentality. When I was younger my family was lower income and when we went to McDonalds my sister and I would literally have to split a cheeseburger. Vacation was going to my grandparents house about two hours away. So if you grew up like that and haven't learned to trust God you can have a scarcity mentality. If you had some rough financial seasons as an adult and haven't learned to trust God you can develop a scarcity mentality.

Check out the graphic of the Scarcity Mentality. God Supplies and **WE CONSUME**. We think it is all for us and we deserve it. That's what our consumer culture tells us. We spend it all and **WE LACK**. Then the emotion that overwhelms us is **WE FEAR** and then the cycle repeats itself.

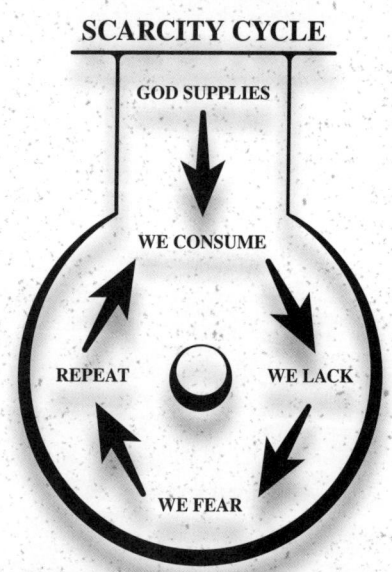

This is how the majority of people in America live. Paycheck to paycheck. God supplies… then we consume, we lack, we fear, we repeat. It's a cycle of scarcity. If you are tense right now, if your butt cheeks tightened up… you might have a little scarcity mentality. I'm just saying. Just relax and breath. Let's talk. I want to show you the mindset that Christ-followers should have. Because of what God did for us through Jesus, it creates a whole different cycle. Not a cycle of scarcity, but a cycle of supply. Paul talked about generosity and breaks down this cycle of supply in 2 Corinthians 9:7, "You must decide in your heart how much to give. And don't give reluctantly or in response to pressure. For God loves a person who gives cheerfully. And God will generously provide all you need. Then you will always have everything you need and plenty left over to share with others. As the scriptures say, 'They share freely and give generously to the poor. Their good deeds will be remembered forever.' For God is the one who provides seed for the farmer and then bread to eat. In the same way, he will provide and increase your resources and then produce a great harvest of generosity in you. Yes, you will be enriched in every way so that you can always be generous. And when we take your gifts to those who need them, they will thank God."

This is exactly what happens through the church. At Crossover Church we have Love Our City week and multiple serving days throughout the year. People are generous and give and God multiplies it as we go out and serve thousands of people in our community. Those people who receive the generosity thank God. We get to literally live out this passage from the Bible. We watch it happen in real life.

> *"God wants us to move from a scarcity mentality to a generosity mentality."*

So when we get our paycheck and God supplies, the first thing we do is WE GIVE some of it. This is actually an act of worship. We give back to the one who supplied it. God was generous with us first as he gave his son Jesus so we could be forgiven and made brand new. We didn't deserve it, we didn't earn it, but God was generous to us. When we give and we put that seed in the ground, what does God do? HE MULTIPLIES it. We don't have to fear like the scarcity mentality. We watch God supernaturally supply and multiply what we have and then WE GROW. We've seen it work and then we repeat.

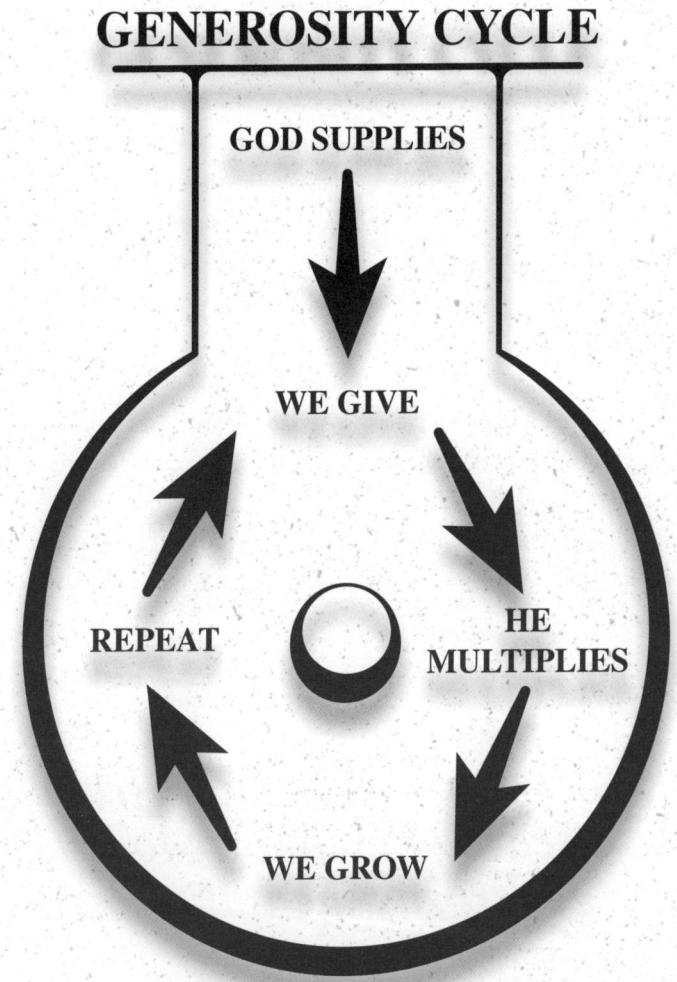

"Give Multiply Grow Repeat"
Urban D. - Love Our City Album

vs. 1

I grew up with the scarcity mentality / Low income - that was my reality / That can crush your dreams like fatality / Cuz you always spending up your whole entire salary / I was stuck in rut / Stuck in the mud / Til Christ intervened - picked me up with his love / I experienced forgiveness & abundance / He broke the cycle of Fear and Redundance /

vs. 2

I'll be honest - it was hard at first / Even though we say we want to put God first / Cuz we all struggle with this material thirst / But we can't take nothing when we get in the hearse / We only get to hold it for a minute / Real easy to spend it - Real hard to give it / It's real hard to live it / But God can take your little and Bridge it / Multiply it double digit / I'm a witness / I learned generosity / It becomes intuitive in God's economy / And now it's all up in me / I get so excited to give back and Love My City / With my church fam - we so saucy / Can't wait til we Multiply with Crossover Coffee / Serving living water from the well / From Tampa Bay to Crossover ATL

Leveling up.

We give, he multiplies, we grow, repeat. Instead of living in fear of lack, we take this crazy leap of faith and we level up and give. It may not seem to make sense, but we do it and we watch God show up. This is what happens when we are generous. We level up. But just saying the word generous can be somewhat vague and general. What does that really mean? How much, how often? How does this really work? I'm grateful that you've read this far along in the book and you are interested in taking your generosity to the next level. It doesn't deal with a certain amount as we are all at different financial levels. $100 to someone might be everything they have, while to someone else it may be like giving 10 cents. It a percentage that makes it level for everyone. Remember I said that the average American only gives 2.8% of their income. God's desire is that we start with giving 10% of our income. In the Bible it is called a "Tithe". It comes from the Hebrew word Mahaser that means a tenth. A tenth of everything God blesses us with, we bring back to him as an act of worship. Some people ask or even argue that it doesn't matter as some of these parts of the Bible were written in the Old Testament under the religious law. But, if you do your research you can find that Abraham brought a tithe to the priest before the law was in place. Then you can also go to the New Testament and find where Jesus affirms tithing in Matthew 23:23. He says, you should tithe, but don't forget the more important matters. In other words, tithing is an assumption… but don't forget love, mercy and grace!

Here are two thoughts about tithing. Maybe you've never heard of it, or you don't know know why we should do it. You might be suspect of it like I was at one point in my life. The first thought is that the tithe teaches us to put God first. Check out Deuteronomy 14:23 where it says tithing will teach you to always have fear (reverence and respect) for God. Many people will regularly say that God is #1 in their lives, but if you look at the evidence of their lives that is not the case. Tithing teaches you to really put him #1 in your life. I know some of you are thinking… if I was going to start tithing regularly I would have to rearrange my whole life around God. Yup… that's the point. It does take crazy faith to go from 2 or 3 percent giving to 10 percent. My family has entirely rearranged our lives and put God first in our finances and I've got stories for days of how God has multiplied and showed up again and again. The second thought about tithing is that it builds our faith. This is what Malachi 3:10-11 shares, "Bring the whole tithe into the storehouse (The local church - God's house), that there may be food in my house. Test me in this,' says the Lord." This is the only place in the Bible where God invites us to Test him! He's saying, try it... and look at the next verse, "And see if I will not throw open the floodgates of heaven and pour out so much blessing that there will not be room enough to store it." This doesn't mean money is going to rain down, but it does mean God will bless you and provide for you. Many times that is in ways that money can't buy... with health, peace and contentment. God is basically saying in this passage, see if my economy is different than the world's. You've already tried Consume, Lack, Fear, Repeat... but have you really tried Give, Multiply, Grow, Repeat?

> *"God is asking us to give our first and best and he will bless the rest."*

The generosity muscle.

Generosity is like a muscle. I work out 2-3 times a week. If I told you to drop down and give me 40 push ups in a row, most of you would probably not be able to do it. Maybe you could do 10 or 20. If you started doing some push ups daily, then next week you probably could do about 4 or 5 more. In a month maybe 15 or 20 more more. In six months you probably could do 40 or pretty close to it. A few years ago on Father's Day we did a push up challenge at our church. I challenged any dad that could beat me would get a $100 gift card. I started training and doing my push ups almost everyday. When it came to the challenge day I did 88 push ups in a row. In the first service the closest person did 65. In the second service there was a guy that was a cross fit competitor that did 99 and in third service a guy that recently got out of prison did 101. It was a lot of fun and it pushed a lot of us to get in better shape. Before the training I could do about 50 in a row, but I pushed myself and grew those muscles to almost double. As you start being generous and giving, you may feel it and get a little sore at first. But, as you grow that generosity muscle and start giving consistently, you get stronger. You'll watch God show up and multiply things and you'll give a little more and get a little stronger in this area of your life. My wife and I started giving 10% of our income and over time we've grown to give away a little more every year. I'm not saying that to brag, but to encourage you that as you give, God will multiply and grow your faith and your resources. Especially as you see how it is changing lives and it's changing your life. As your heart changes you'll realize that it really is more blessed to give than to receive.

There were also seasons where we were faithful in giving our tithes and additional offering above that and things would still get tight. Our margins would get depleted and our savings got low. We still had everything we needed, but it got really tight. Those are testing moments. We can be tempted to cut back our giving or stop altogether, but we stayed consistent. We always watched God come through. We never told anybody, but people would bless us with something we needed. There were four years in a row where we got to take a vacation that was paid for by an organization or an individual. We were worn out doing urban ministry sixty to seventy hours a week, but we didn't have any extra money to go away. God would open up a miracle door. My wife and I were even blessed to go to Hawaii for one whole week on a marriage retreat at this five star resort. All expenses paid. It was a trip we will never forget. It strengthened our marriage and our faith.

Less is more.

Our culture programs us to think that more is always better. Bigger is better. Let's super size it! When I was a kid my parents gave me a piggy bank and I'd save all of my spare change and sometimes dump it out and play with it. Eventually my piggy bank filled up and my parents took me to the bank to change it out for some bills. I traded in a big pile of change and got back a $20 bill and I was upset. At first I couldn't understand the exchange as I turned in a pile of all of these coins and I only got back one piece of paper. I thought I was getting ripped off, I didn't understand that many times… less is more.

King Solomon was the richest man that ever lived. Historians estimate he was about ten times richer than Jeff Bezos (Amazon's owner). He wrote this little book in the Old Testament called Ecclesiastes. It was written near the end of his life as he reflected on all of his accomplishments and his riches. God used him to write some incredible sobering wisdom. In Ecclesiastes 4:6 he said, "Better is one handful with tranquility than two handfuls with toil and chasing after the wind."

> *"It boils down to having less of what doesn't matter so I can have more of what does."*

So you have to ask yourself, what really matters? Let me help you frame it in. Imagine you only had one month left to live. What would you do? What would really matter at that point? What is the most important? I posted that question up on Facebook a couple of years ago and I had dozens of responses. Nobody said it was their money. Nobody said it was how great their sneaker collection was or how many designer purses they had. Nobody talked about their car. Nobody said how many social media followers they had. People said what really mattered was my family, my friends, my legacy and my relationship with God. If that is really true, why do we spend so much of our lives pursuing things that don't even make the "Most important list". This is why we need God to continue to change our hearts and make them more like his.

The first thing we need to learn to do is "Cut Back". If you have ever been to an older house you will find that most of them didn't have many closets. Many bedrooms had no closets and if they did, they were really small. Why was this? Because back in the day people had a lot less clothes and stuff. Fast forward to today and now we have closets in every room and some of you could make your master bedroom closet into another bedroom it's so large. And yet, many of us will walk into our closets packed full of clothes and stare and stare and say, "I've got nothing to…" Yes, I know you were able to finish that sentence because you've said it before. Some of us have so much stuff we have to put some in the garage. Some of you have so much stuff you can't even park your car in your garage anymore. Then there are many people that have so much stuff in their closets, garages and attics that they have to rent a storage unit. One of the biggest industries that has grown in the past few decades is the storage industry. They just built a huge four story storage facility just down the street from our church. It towers over the small buildings in front of it. Here is how it works… you pay someone to store your stuff that you never see and you don't use and you probably forgot you even have it. Remember what King Solomon said? Better is one hand with tranquility than two hands with a bunch of stress and stuff.

The second thing we need to do is "Clear Out" some things. Some of you may have grown up like me where you didn't have as much. We had to conserve things and make sure we weren't wasting anything. We didn't throw things out often. On the other hand many of us have some things that have sentimental value. But, like Ecclesiastes tells us, one handful can be peaceful and two handfuls can become stressful. Why do we go into our packed closets and say we have nothing to wear?

"We have too many options."

Have you ever went on Netflix and couldn't decide what movie or show to watch? Too many options. But, when I've been on a long plane flight with only 8 movies to choose from, I'll watch 3 of them. When I go to Cheesecake Factory I usually struggle. The food is pretty good, but I can't decide on what to order as there are so many pages to the menu. When I go to In and Out Burger it's easy because they just have burgers, fries and shakes. When you cut back and you clear out it becomes easier on your heart and soul to make choices. Some of us need to go through our closets and clear a bunch of stuff out that we don't use. Be generous and take it and bless someone else.

The third way we can realize that less is more is to "Pay Off". We all know that financial stress is not fun. I've never had anyone tell me that their debt makes them peaceful. But, I have had people tell me that their generosity makes them full of joy. Let me again refer to King Solomon's words and remix them.

Better is a car that is paid off than two brand new cars with stressful payments. Better is a smaller house filled with love than a bigger one filled with fights and arguments. Better is financial margin and being able to help others than living paycheck to paycheck and worrying that if the paycheck stopped everything could collapse. As your heart begins to change you begin to look at all of your finances and resources differently. The next step is to make new choices as we realize less can really be more. Then we begin to watch our situation change.

Watch "Your Heart Changes" video @
www.youtube.com/urband813

Heart Changes:

1. In what ways has God been changing your heart?

2. Have you ever chased after treasure and watched things fall apart?

3. Did you realize how rich you are? In what way?

4. Did you grow up in the Scarcity Cycle or the Generosity Cycle? Where are you at today?

5. What are some ways you could workout your Generosity Muscle?

6. How can you "Cut Back" and "Clear Out" some things to make your life simpler?

7. What are some goals of things you want to "Pay Off".

CHAPTER 2

It changes your Situation.

God changes our heart when we become more generous. The next thing that begins to happen is that our situation begins to change. There was a woman that grew to have a heart of generosity, but was still struggling financially. She heard about this outreach mission but only had a little over $5 in her bank account. She wrote a check for her last $5, but was embarrassed at the small amount. She prayed that God would take it and multiply it. She went to her small group Bible study from her church that night. After the group, a couple approached her and said they had been praying and that God made it clear that they were supposed to give her something. They handed her an envelope with a check in it for $1,000. God doesn't always work like this, but He can and He does. I've seen many stories like this happen where God will radically change someone's situation in just one moment.

Many of us hear a story like that and can think, "I would love for somebody to give me a check for $1,000." We can easily think of all the things we could do with that money. But, what if we looked at it differently and said, "God, I wish I was in a situation where I could be the one that could give the $1,000!" Wow. Drop the mic.

> *"Many times we look at situations through the wrong lenses. When our heart truly becomes more generous we see through new lenses."*

Then God begins to change our situation so we can become even more generous.

Situations change.

Nicole was working a job that could be considered a toxic environment. One day her boss called her into her office and announced she was being fired. The reason had no validity, but at the same time she was relieved to be released from all the drama. However, financially this was devastating news. She had a mortgage to pay and it would be several weeks before unemployment kicked in. A few months prior she had to replace her entire HVAC system in her house and she was left was very little savings to fall back on. Yet she continued to be faithful in her giving and she experienced God's generosity. She quickly decided to put her house on the market. Nicole bought her house for $112,000 and the first weekend she put the house on the market there were 26 showings and 6 offers. The house ended up selling for $139,500. God flipped the entire situation. She remained faithful during this time as she still tithed and was generous even from her unemployment checks. But it didn't stop there. She soon got a new job in a much healthier environment and she was making more money. She moved closer to her family and she started attending Transformation Church which is in the Charlotte area.

In the summer of 2018 I went to speak at Transformation Church as Pastor Derwin Gray is a good friend of mine. Nicole was there and was touched. She started watching Crossover Church online and God began to move on her heart and led her to move to Tampa as she felt so connected to the tribe at Crossover. The money she made off of her first house being sold was the seed money to buy her home in Tampa. Nicole points to Romans 8:28 and how God works all things for the good. It didn't feel good to lose her job and then have to quickly pack up and sell her house, but God was putting all the pieces of the puzzle together for her future. She attributes this to being faithful with little and God blessing her with more as she continued to be generous in her giving even when times were rocky. Today Nicole serves with the Chosen Women's ministry and is enjoying her new life in Tampa with her new church family.

In 2006 I met Ed. He invited me to lunch as he was the chairman of the Luis Palau Festival that was coming to Tampa. He heard from multiple people that I was the guy to talk to about creating a Hip-Hop stage at the event. It was an awesome opportunity that allowed us to touch tens of thousands of people. I was able to perform and curate the line up of artists for the Hip-Hop and Extreme Sports stage. But, it wasn't just a transactional encounter, a real relationship was built over the next several years. I learned so many things from Ed. His family opened their home several times to me, my wife and my daughters. I also brought several groups of young men that I was mentoring to come hear his story at his house. At the time he lived in a beautiful home on the bay with an incredible view. Several of the guys I brought over were from the inner-city and never had stepped foot in a house like that before. It was fun to watch their reaction, but it was even more fun to watch them when Ed told his story. It would be easy to step in a home like that and assume that he came from a rich family, but his story was the total opposite.

He grew up poor as an only child with his mom. His mother was the mistress of a married guy that had another family. His father had promised to leave his wife and marry Ed's mom, but that never happened. Eventually he was totally out of the picture and they were on their own. Ed started working at a very young age everyday after school so he could help his mom with some of the bills. After High School he went into the military and thought that would be his life. Eventually he left the military and got into real estate. He quickly became very successful at it, but he was far from God. The economy crashed and he and his young wife lost everything. Instead of declaring bankruptcy, he worked for many years to pay off all of his debts. As he rebuilt his company and finances, he found Christ and everything started rebuilding the right way.

"When his heart changed his generosity grew and his situation changed."

He built a successful real estate company for many years. All this time, he knew who his real father was and one day in his business dealings he met his half brother. His half brother had the same first name as Ed and didn't even know he had a brother. They were so happy to be united that his half brother invited him to come and run his company in Tampa.

Since Ed has been in Tampa he has changed that company and he has changed the spiritual climate of business in our city. He has influenced hundreds of business leaders through his Bible Studies, leadership classes and personal mentorship. His radical generosity has helped fund several ministries and fund several large events and spiritual initiatives. Ed and his development company were instrumental in helping our church acquire our building from Toys R' Us in 2010. Ed grew up as a poor kid in Pittsburgh, but God got a hold of his heart and everything changed. He is truly one of the most generous people that I personally know.

My situation has dramatically changed since I first got married. My wife and I made a decision to always tithe and be generous. This was challenging during some lean seasons, but we watched God always provide. My family was lower-income until I was in my later years of high school, so when we traveled to visit family we always drove. I never had been on a plane until I was 19 years old. A few years into being married I was on planes regularly to travel around the country to do music and share my story. My wife was able to occasionally travel with me as well. Soon a passport became necessary and over the years I've been on over a dozen international trips. Who would have thought that this kid from Philly would be touring around the world? God changed our situation because of our generosity in our time, talent and treasure. He had blessed me with an entrepreneurial mind to write books, music and curriculum. He has blessed me with opportunities to speak at churches, events and conferences. Over 100 pastors have been trained through my urban pastors masterclass. All of this has created other streams of income to not only provide for my family, but also for my family to give like never before. In 2018 we started our own publishing company "Tranzlation Leadership". This book was published through our company and 100% of the proceeds of this book are going to Crossover Church and Love Our City. Our situation has changed and we're blessed to be a blessing.

Two legs.

It takes two legs to walk. Most of us would say we want to live a life that is blessed by God. When it comes to our finances we need two legs to walk a blessed path: Generosity and Management. Let me frame it in like this… if you are generous, but you are also a terrible manager and spend on whatever, your finances will still be a hot mess. Why would God bless you when you are going to waste so much of it? On the other hand, if you are a good manager, but you are not generous, why would God bless you either? Here's a newsflash: God's purpose is to get the resources to the people who need it. Think about all the needs in our world. There are people that need food, water, shelter and most of all they need to hear the message about Jesus. God has the supplies to handle all of this. How does he meet needs? Through people.

> *"God funnels his resources through his people."*

But, if your funnel gets clogged up, he can use someone else. He wants us to be a river, not a reservoir.

I've had a few injuries playing basketball over the years. I sprained my ankle a few times when I was in high school and college. In 2016 I ruptured my achilles and had to get surgery to repair it. I have since retired from my favorite sport. During those injuries I had to use crutches because I couldn't walk with one of my legs. In the same way there are so many people that are financially walking with crutches because one of their legs isn't working properly. Either they are generous and the management leg is injured, or they are good managers and the generosity leg is broken. When one leg is down you aren't able to walk in financial freedom. God's desire is for us to have two healthy financial legs that are balanced and working together.

Management situation.

There are several scriptures in the Bible that talk about managing our money. The Bible doesn't just talk about what to do with 10% of your money, it has lots of principles on what to do with all 100% of it. Proverbs 27 says we should know the state of our flocks (our possessions and assets) and reminds us that riches won't last forever. Luke chapter 14 shares about counting the cost and planning ahead. The book of wisdom reminds us about debt and says,

> *"Just as the rich rule the poor,
> so the borrower is servant to the lender."*
> *- Proverbs 22:7*

As we grow in our relationship with God and our generosity increases we also need to apply new management skills to our finances. God wants us to be good stewards of all of our money. This can be challenging as we live in a consumer culture. We live in a world that regularly lives beyond its means.

Many Individuals, families, companies and governments spend more than they bring in. Unfortunately this has become the norm. We all know it's not sustainable. It just doesn't add up. Debt is weighing so many people down.

Debt can be a natural generosity blocker. I regularly meet a lot of people that want to be generous, but they are upside-down in their finances. I believe you can start to be generous in some capacity no matter what your bank account looks like. But having a balanced budget can definitely allow you more freedom to be generous. Achieving a balanced budget takes discipline and intentionality. The first baby step is listing out all of your monthly income and your bills. You may discover you have more month left than you do money. You may have to cut some things out (different services or luxuries). You also may need to create some additional streams of income (do some over-time at work, or pick up a second job, or Uber a few days a week). There are lots of options in today's gig economy to gain some extra money. Of course the temptation is that when more comes in, you can end up spending more. You have to be super disciplined to use that extra money to pay down debt, or save or for whatever bill you have designated it for. The next step is to save up an emergency fund. Many experts say $1,000 is a good start. This is for when something breaks or some type of emergency pops up. It will keep you from putting it on a credit card or borrowing it from someone.

There are many great resources, books and podcasts that can help you work on your management skills and consistency. Some books I recommend are: Financial Peace by Dave Ramsey, The Treasure Principle by Randy Alcorn, Beyond Blessed by Robert Morris and Money, Possessions and Eternity by Randy Alcorn. One management tip...

"I always stress to invest in the things that appreciate."

Our culture regularly invests in things that depreciate like cars, clothes and technology. So many people strive to have the latest and greatest. But, wise stewards will invest in things that grow over time, such as a house, real estate and other solid investments. These are things that can passively grow. They can be passed onto your family and create opportunities for the next generation to continue your legacy of generosity.

Situational giving.

As God changes our heart, he puts us in different situations where we can respond by giving in different ways. Here are 3 ways we can give faithfully in different situations:

1. Give Spontaneously

This is when you see a need and you can meet it. God has given you time and resources and you can meet needs when they pop up. This is the way that most people give. A natural disaster happens and it's unexpected, but there are people that will jump in and give. When there was a hurricane in Houston a few years ago, our church spontaneously gave. When another storm hit the Bahamas we collected a couple tons of food and supplies to ship over. In 2017 Hurricane Irma hit us in Tampa and most of our community lost power for up to a week. We had to cancel church that Sunday as the storm was hitting, so we were short on our weekly budget. But, even in our lack we immediately set up a Hurricane Relief effort at the church. We fed hot meals and gave out groceries and bottled waters every night that week. How were we able to afford that being that we were already short? Other churches and donors from around the country that are our friends spontaneously jumped in and generously gave. In Matthew chapter 14 Jesus was teaching out in a remote area and there were thousands and thousands of people attending. The message went a little long and the disciples were trying to get Jesus to end the service and let people go back to the villages to eat. But, watch what Jesus said in verse 16, "That isn't necessary, you feed them." How could they do that? There were so many people. The miracle all started with a little boy that had Hebrew Hot Pockets of two loaves and five fish. The disciples said they needed some food. He saw the need and spontaneously gave his lunch.

"He simply gave what he had."

He spontaneously gave, God multiplied and did a miracle and not only were thousands of people fed, but there were leftovers! #doggiebags

I have a friend named Rob Clay who is also known as Big Rob. He got the nickname because he is 6 foot 10 inches tall. He is a big man! Rob has a size 18 shoe. You can imagine it is not easy to find shoes and they are not cheap. Several years ago he was desperately in need of getting some new shoes and he was praying that God would provide a way. Rob is married with 4 kids, so there are lots of other shoes to buy. He went to church that day and someone came up to him and gave him a gift card. They shared with him that the Lord told them to give them this gift card from a shoe store so he could get some new sneakers. This person spontaneously gave and it answered Rob's prayer. Inside he was jumping for joy, because he really needed some new kicks. As soon as he walked away, God spoke to him and told him to give the gift card away to another guy that was across the room. Rob started to argue with God for a second saying, "Wait, this is for my shoes, I prayed for it and you know I needed it, and you answered my prayer." God spoke to Rob and told him that the other guy needed it even more. Rob was wrestling with it in his head. Then he felt God speak to him and tell him,

> **"If you trust me, you will never have to buy sneakers again, unless you want to."**

Rob was obedient and spontaneously gave the gift card away. The guy receiving it almost broke down in tears as he really needed shoes. Rob felt blessed that he could give it and soon forgot about it. Rob is a singer and a few weeks later he was invited to sing the national anthem at the OKC Thunder game. Kevin "KD" Durant was playing for the team at the time and his manager pulled Big Rob aside and told him that KD wanted to meet him. They got to talk and it was real cool. KD's asked him what size his shoes were. Then he told his manager to get his information. The manager called him a few days later and told him to meet him at a certain location. Rob pulled up, not knowing what to expect. The manager opened up the back of his SUV and had dozens of boxes of KD's Nike sneakers in size 18 for him. If you've ever seen the KD brand, they are some really cool, unique sneakers that can easily run $200 a pair. Here is a fun fact - many of these KD's that Big Rob got were prototypes that Nike made just for KD to see if he liked the certain colors and styles. Several were never even released! These were like collectors items. This happened several more times where KD's manager would call Rob and tell him to bring his SUV as he was going to fill it up with sneakers. Over time he received hundreds of pairs of KD's and Nike Air Force One's. Rob still has a couple dozen pairs, but he was able to spontaneously give away hundreds of these pairs to students that he would meet that had big feet. Remember what God told Big Rob? Be obedient and give this gift card and you will never buy sneakers again, unless you want to. Wow.

Pastor Tommy & Big Rob

2. The second way to give is Strategically.

Many of us can hear those spontaneous giving stories and say, "I'd want to give like that, but I can't." Well, you can if you plan. If your heart changes and you shift from the Scarcity mentality to the Generosity mentality and you start planning. Your situation will change. Many of us give last to God. We need to strategically flip that and learn to give first to God. Plan to put God first in every area of your life. Don't just give when you feel like it, or you have it, but give as an act of worship. Isaiah 32:8 says, "But generous people plan to do what is generous, and they stand firm in their generosity."

"Most of us are good planners with our money… we plan to spend it!"

We see something we want and we save up to buy it, or we borrow money or charge it. We figure out how to spend our money. Why can't we do that same thing with giving? Sometimes we have to save up to give a strategic gift. We have to cut some things so we can give a little more. We have to be intentional. God wants us to move from consumers to become contributors.

My wife and I have rearranged some things in our lives so we can strategically give our tithe to our church and in addition give regular offerings above that to our church and also to some other ministries and missionaries that we are passionate about. We can't do any of those things unless we plan it, because life happens. We have two teenage daughters and the money can disappear quickly. We have to be strategic. I love the story of Pastor Rick Warren. He has been a friend of our church for several years and their ministry has helped us many times in many ways. When he first wrote the Purpose Driven Life it blew up and it was on the New York Times best seller list for a long time. He knew he was going to have some big royalty checks coming his way soon. Rick and his wife sat down and made a commitment not to change their personal lifestyle. They already had a nice house and were comfortable. God had already blessed them in so many ways. So, they planned to give most of the book money away. When he got the first large royalty check he had been the Pastor at Saddleback Church for 20 years. He added up all the money that his salary had been from the church all of those years and wrote a check to the church and gave it all back! Rick then told the church he was also taking himself off salary from the church and that he would work for free moving forward. Then as the book money kept coming in and kept multiplying, he kept giving more and more. He and his wife decided to become reverse tithers. What is that? They give away 90% of their income and live off of 10%. They started several foundations to help Aids victims in Africa and they help plant churches. One of Pastor Rick's foundations made a donation that helped our church when we first got in our building. How can he and his wife do that? They are strategic. Now, you and I may never have a best selling book, but we can be strategic with what we do have and become generous givers and watch God multiply it!

3. The third way to give is *Sacrificially*.

This way of giving will really change your situation. There are so many powerful examples of sacrificial giving in the scriptures. One that really stands out to me is found in Mark's Gospel. It's where Jesus is sitting in the temple watching what people were giving. This is how Mark told the story in Mark chapter 12 starting in verse 41, "Jesus sat down near the collection box in the

Temple and watched as the crowds dropped in their money. Many rich people put in large amounts. Then a poor widow came and dropped in two small coins. Jesus called his disciples to him and said, 'I tell you the truth, this poor widow has given more than all the others who are making contributions. For they gave a tiny part of their surplus, but she, poor as she is, has given everything she had to live on.'" Jesus didn't stop this poor woman. He wasn't like, "Hey, don't worry about it, the rich people got it covered…" No, he didn't rob her from her blessing of giving and he celebrated her sacrificial gift. We're still talking about it today.

When is the last time you received the blessing of giving sacrificially? When you gave and you really felt it? And you loved that you gave up something to be a massive blessing to someone else? A few years ago our church did a special offering for several new ways our church was going to multiply to reach more people. We were expanding our outreach week "Love Our City" from 70 community service projects to over 100 community service projects to reach over 10,000 people. We were starting plans to work on our coffee shop in our lobby and we announced that we were going to launch our second location (Crossover Church ATL) in the city of Atlanta. These were all amazing initiatives that were going to help our church multiply our impact for God. My wife and I prayed and planned on how to give in the most sacrificial way our family ever had. My mother had passed away about six months earlier. My parents didn't have a whole lot. My mother didn't become a homeowner until she was in her 60's. She had purchased a little townhouse and we were so proud of her. My sister and I put her townhouse on the market and it sold in a few months. The equity money was basically our inheritance. My sister and I split it. My wife and I had strategic plans for our half of the money. But, God spoke to us and told us to give it. It would be the best investment we could ever make. I sacrificially gave my inheritance so God could multiply it and help others find their spiritual inheritance. When we build a relationship with Christ, we get adopted into his family and we gain a spiritual inheritance of eternal life, blessing and all kinds of incredible things we don't deserve.

Watch "Your Situation Changes" Video @
www.youtube.com/urband813

Pastor Tommy and his mom "Yaya"

Situational Changes:

1. If you've implemented generosity, how has your situation changed?

2. Do you know someone's situation that has changed?

3. How has the way you manage money changed?

4. Have you ever given spontaneously?

5. Have you ever been strategic about giving? What is your current strategy?

6. Have you ever given sacrificially? How did that feel?

7. What ways are you praying your current situation will change?

CHAPTER 3

It changes your Church.

The elephant.

Let's address the elephant in the room: "A church talking about money." Yes, I said it! This can bring a mixed bag of emotions for so many people. Unfortunately, the church has not always done a good job talking about it or being transparent with it. Then there are a few churches out there that have really messed up in this area. But at the same time there are countless churches doing incredible work in their communities and making a difference in the lives of so many people. But, those are rarely the churches that we see talked about on the news. The ones highlighted are usually those that had a scandal with money or the pastor had a moral failure. If you've experienced this first hand it can cause you to lose trust in the church as a whole. You may even question if you want to ever give to a church again. I understand. I grew up in church and have seen the good, the bad and the ugly. On the other hand you may have been at a church where they constantly talked about money and pressured people to give more. There are also some churches that lack transparency and never talk about what happens with any of the resources and if you ask about it they question your loyalty to God.

Those are some of the things that made me run from my calling to be involved in church ministry. When I finally submitted to God and accepted my calling to lead in a local church I had some conditions. These weren't conditions for God, they were for me and the church I would help lead. I wanted to be part of a church that was diverse. It wasn't going to be a Hispanic Church or a Black church or a White Church. It was going to be a church where everyone was welcomed, no matter what their skin color or ethnic background was. But, I had also seen some ethnically diverse churches that had no economic diversity. I dreamt about having a church where poor people sat right next to wealthy people and middle class people sat in… you know the middle. Just wanted to make sure you were still tracking with me, but seriously, I wanted to create a church that was multi-class. A place where people of different economic backgrounds could be family and empower one another and learn from one another. In addition I wanted to strip down all of the man-made traditions and creatively teach and preach the Bible in context. I wanted a church that was huge on community outreach and was known for loving our city. When it came to money there needed to be great systems, great management and great transparency.

Crossover Church is not perfect, but we have become a thriving multi-ethnic, multi-generational, multi-class church. We disciple people to live life in 3D (Discover, Develop and Display their life in Christ) and we love our city well. When it comes to our finances and resources I can confidently say we have great systems in place. It is multi-layered for accountability. Our church has a finance team that processes all the donations given physically and digitally. Physical money is always counted by multiple people together and they each sign forms with the totals. We have a book keeper that reconciles everything into our quickbooks and does all of our bill pay. We then have a certified CPA that double checks our books quarterly. In addition we have several individuals in our leadership team that have online access to look at our accounts and see everything that is happening. We also have great management in place as our Church Council of elders meets monthly to make major spiritual and financial decisions. Our Executive Team meets weekly with our book keeper to strategize what is happening with the immediate details of the budget. We strive to maximize every dollar to make it have the greatest impact for God's work.

Great transparency is very important to us as we produce an annual ministry report. This report celebrates our ministry impact with numbers and stories. It shares how much money was donated and how it was used. We present this in our Sunday Services in the spring and then we publicly post it on our website and youtube channel. This is not something that churches are legally required to do, but I would suggest that every church would go above and beyond and produce an annual report. We transparently show people how their generosity is making a direct impact on people's lives. I believe the days of people blindly giving to an organization are over. This generation wants accountability and transparency.

> **Your church's capacity changes.**

When I first became the lead pastor in 2002 there were around 40 people attending on Sundays and most of them were under 30 years old (including myself). One thing our church always had was a passion to reach people for Christ. But, as you can imagine, we had a much smaller capacity than our church does today. We were much smaller in number, not nearly as mature and our generosity muscle was not very developed. My wife and I were personally tithing and giving, but I had never taught on the subject before. Talking about money in a church setting made me very uncomfortable. This is because at the time there were other larger churches in our city that were known for always talking about money, pressuring people and taking up multiple offerings in one church service. Some of them were regularly preaching what is known as the "Prosperity Gospel." If you aren't familiar with that term, it's basically if you give more money, God will bless you with more for you and your dreams. This teaching will say things like, "If you want a bigger house or a fancy sports car, you need to plant your seed here and God will supernaturally give you what you want. You deserve it. You need to claim it. It's yours!" This is not Biblical and it ends up leaving a lot of people hurt and confused. Several people over the years started coming to Crossover from those environments and they found it refreshing that that was not the message we were preaching. I regularly would hear this from people. So at first this caused me to want to avoid talking about money altogether because I didn't want to get lumped in with those other types of churches.

But, as I continued to grow as a pastor and a leader, I knew I had to also talk about money. Why? Because money, possessions and generosity are addressed throughout the Bible.

"If I was going to be a good pastor, I had to teach the entire Bible, not just the parts I was comfortable with."

The difference is that I was going to make sure I was teaching it in context in a balanced way. The scripture has so many helpful things to say about financial management and generosity. The very first time I taught a series on money was in 2005. Yes, it took me a few years to study, pray and research how some other solid churches were teaching on these important topics. I still have the notes from the series. As I was writing this, I dug into my archives and found them. It was called "On Track". We creatively used the analogy of our lives being like a subway car and how our money, possessions and materialism can quickly get us off track if we don't stay connected to the 3rd rail which is God our power source. The series connected with our church on a deep level. For many the light turned on. They were learning about generosity and managing their money in a way like they had never heard before. The series shared several Biblical stories about Abraham and Cain and Abel. I taught the series with some other leaders. We each shared what we were learning about generosity. Our church was growing together and God was expanding our capacity.

In 2005 our church was located at our old campus behind the Tampa Zoo. It was a small building that could barely seat 200 people if we packed in the chairs from the edge of the stage to the back wall. At that time we were preparing to launch a 3rd service time and complete an overflow patio on the backside of the church. Our capacity was growing as our people were becoming more generous with their time, their talent and their treasure. God was doing something special at that little church building in the middle of a neighborhood. As a matter of fact, soon after we started that 3rd service and opened up the overflow patio we were maxed out of space again. We needed more room to reach more people as our passion to lead them to Christ was continuing to grow.

Crossover's former N. Orleans Campus

In the fall of 2008 we casted vision about moving to the former Toys R' Us building on Fowler Ave. (Our current Uptown Tampa location). We had a special Sunday at the AMC Movie theaters and gathered all 3 of our services together at one time. We launched our Growth Campaign to help raise funds to make the big move. It was exciting and scary all at the same time. It was a terrible time to ask anyone to give extra money due to the fact that our country was entering the "Great Recession". But, our people's capacity of faith and trust in God had grown and people stepped up and sacrificially gave. We were amazed at people's generosity. It was because their capacity had changed. Our church was radically different than it was just three years earlier. My generosity as the pastor had also radically grown. Like I shared my wife and I had already been faithfully tithing, but we had never given a large sacrificial offering before. That was new for us. Things were tight, and we didn't have anything extra to give. But, I was hopeful that God would open some additional doors for me to go out and speak and do music at other events and churches. I already was consistently doing that as the extra income I made from speaking helped pay some of our bills. Now, I was going to go out even more to raise money for the growth campaign. It was like I was getting a second, no, actually a third job. God gave me the ability to trust him and as I did, he opened up new opportunities and provided the capacity for me to be sacrificially generous. I did a tour called the "Growth Tour". Over the next eighteen months I was able to give over $15,000 towards our new building. People saw me and my family modeling sacrificial giving and they followed along. Several people changed spending habits and some picked up more hours at their job so they could give extra.

Over the next two years we raised over half a million dollars for us to relocate to the former Toys R' Us building. We also sold our previous location which enabled us to have enough money to rebuild the inside of the building. It was basically an empty shell. We had to do all the plumbing, bathrooms, walls, electrical, lights, air conditioning and much more. It was a massive project. I would have never dreamt our church could take on the task of rebuilding a 43,000 square foot facility. But God! He increased our capacity as our hearts were generous. Rebuilding the building would mean rebuilding people's lives in the neighborhood. Many churches that invest over a million dollars on a new building go to the suburbs or a nicer part of the city. We did the opposite.

> *"We felt like God was calling us
> to go where the greatest needs were."*

So, we went from more of a middle class neighborhood at our old location to a very challenged neighborhood at our new one. The old nickname for the community was "Suitcase City". It was known for its transient nature with high eviction rates and homelessness. We felt God brought us there to help change the atmosphere. We came to bring stability and hope. There are still many challenges in our neighborhood, but it is changing! We have shed our old nickname and our community has become an Innovation District that is now known as Uptown.

Your church's influence changes.

Our church had the grand opening in our new facility on Sunday November 7th, 2010. We had over 1,300 people attend and over 100 people started a relationship with Christ. We only had the capacity to accommodate half as many people at our old location. Our church was now in this large building on a main street that has 60,000 cars pass by each day. Our old location only had a few hundred cars see us daily. Our influence immediately changed. Dozens of first time guests were coming to our services just because they drove by and noticed it. So many people were checking out our website it moved to the first page of google when you search for churches in Tampa. This caused even more people to find us. All of this happened because a small army of people became generous and said, "We need to rebuild our city," "We need more space so we can make more disciples", "We will do whatever it takes!" Our influence continues to grow as we change our community. You'll read the details about this in the final chapter… keep going, it's about to get really good!

> **Your church's impact changes.**

In 1979 there was a prophecy given at our old building that the church would impact the city, the state, the nation and the world. That seemed almost impossible as it was a small church of less than one hundred people. During the 1980's the church actually got smaller and smaller and eventually the pastor left. There were only a few older people left. One of those people was Gordon Meetze. He believed that this prophecy about the church's impact was a message from God, even though the church had basically fallen apart. He and his wife were the last remaining board members on the deed of the property. People told them to give it up and let it go, but Gordon held on as he believed God was going to fulfill that word that was given. In 1991 Gordon met Pastor Joe McCutchen who had just started this church called Crossover. They needed a place to meet. This small group of people started meeting at that little building and a new church was birthed. In 1996 I came and launched the youth ministry. I shared some of those early years at the beginning of the book. The crazy thing is that our church's impact was always larger than our size. Even when we were reaching hundreds of unchurched teens from the urban community we had a very small budget, but a couple dozen young adult leaders that were generous with their time and God blessed it.

As that generosity grew, our impact continued to grow. I shared that I started doing music when I first got to the church. A few years later I signed a national record deal. My CD's were released in stores across the country (Remember when we had to go to stores to buy music? LOL). This created a national platform and impact. Inside of my CD cover I had a picture of our youth ministry with a paragraph talking about our Hip-Hop concerts, basketball league, break dancing classes and other unique programs. Suddenly we had people calling us, emailing us and visiting us from all over the country. Over the next few years there were magazines, TV stations and newspapers that featured the unique work we were doing. MTV even tried to get us to do a reality show. Our church was featured in USA Today, Newsweek, BET News, TBN and several local media outlets. Some of these articles are framed on our history wall at the church. It was funny because I regularly had people asking me who did our PR (Public Relations), I would laugh and say "Jesus!". It was God's favor as our church had a heart of generosity. Our church was not afraid to get uncomfortable and reach unchurched teenagers and adults that didn't always know how to act in church.

In the year 2000 we launched a leadership conference called "Flavor Fest". It was created for pastors, youth pastors, church leaders and artists from the city. We had workshops and general sessions during the day and Hip-Hop concerts in the evening. The first year we had about 300 people attend throughout the weekend. Fast forward 10 years and the weekend of 10/10/10 we celebrated our 10 year anniversary the very weekend we moved to our new location. This time we had over 3,000 people attend. Our impact was 10 times the size in just 10 years. It was epic. People came from all over the world to see what God was doing in this innovative church in Tampa. The prophecy from 1979 may have taken decades to come to pass, but it has truly been fulfilled. Gordon and his family stayed and became part of this new church. The former property was already paid off and Crossover was able to rent it for $1 a year. I'm not sure if we ever actually paid that, but eventually Gordon generously signed over the property to Crossover Church. In 2010 we sold that property and the money was used to help our church level up and come to the former Toys R' Us building. Gordon also had a construction business and worked on the new building as one of the foremen. In 2017 he went home to be the Lord. He was 80 years old. We dedicated the facility to him as we honor his sacrifice, faith and generosity. We are all part of his legacy.

Some of you reading this are from Crossover Church or you recently started attending, but many of you are from another church. Think about the story of your church. How has God blessed their generosity? Our church didn't always have an amazing story. It took time to develop as we matured and grew. Maybe you are still in that process, but I want you to begin to be aware of what God is doing. Many times when we are in the middle of something good, we can take it for granted. We may not even notice the hand of God working. I encourage you to step back and think about your church's impact. If there are generous people there, God will expand your impact. Some of this can be from strategy, but some of it is supernatural. There are many moments of favor that our church experienced that we cannot explain. I can sum it up by saying God has blessed our generosity and has blown our mind with the impact he has given us.

Watch "Your Church Changes" Video @
www.youtube.com/urband813

Church Changes:

1. Have you ever been part of a church where money was mismanaged? If so, How did that make you feel?

2. Have you ever been part of a church that you watched their capacity grow? What happened?

3. What story stuck out to you the most in this chapter?

4. Do people in your community know about your church? Why or why not?

5. Fun Fact: Can you name 5 artists that have been at Flavor Fest?

CHAPTER 4

It changes your City.

Generosity is changing our community. Why? Because the people of God are here and we are shifting the atmosphere. That's what should happen when we learn to follow the words of Jesus in Matthew 22:39 where he says, "love your neighbor as yourself." We quickly noticed many of our neighbors were in need as the poverty level was around 30% in the immediate neighborhood. Our church sprung into action and held our very first Back 2 School Jam in 2009. We hosted it in the parking lot of our building when it was still abandoned. In faith we were already claiming the property and that we were going to start rebuilding the people even before any physical construction started. We hosted a big Hip-Hop Concert and gave away 300 backpacks and told them about our church that was praying about taking over the building. Lives were touched that day in the parking lot. People came to know Jesus! Seven months later we signed the deal. In 2010 we hosted our second annual Back 2 School Jam in the parking lot again, but this time the inside of the building was in the middle of our massive rebuilding project.

> *"Over the past decade we've blessed children of our community with over 10,000 backpacks filled with school supplies."*

We've hosted block parties and given away tons of groceries at events that connected people with dozens of resource partners to help them level up. These were beautiful events where hundreds of our church members generously gave their time and talent to share the love of God in a tangible way. This began to build a relationship of trust with our community as we met needs with no strings attached. Urban ministry legend Bill Wilson said, "They don't care how much you know, until they know how much you care."

Love Our City.

In 2017 we launched one of our largest community changing initiatives called "Love Our City." I gathered our leadership team and told them my dream to have 500 people volunteer in a week at 50 different community service projects. At first there was some push back since we've never had 500 people volunteer for one thing before. We had 300 volunteers at our conference and that seemed really huge, but 500? The other big question was what would these 50 projects consist of and how could we even think of that many? We pulled out the white board and starting listing who lives and works within a 3-4 mile radius of our church campus. It is a very diverse area; College students (USF is less than 2 miles up the street with close to 50k students), business people, young families, single moms, people in poverty, homeless people, immigrants, seniors and several more. Then we started creating projects that would reach each one of those demographics. If we are going to love our city, we want to love ALL of our city, not just one group of people. We creatively came up with different ways to touch each tribe. There are 3 main categories of projects: service projects, pay it forward and appreciation lunches. Service projects consist of cutting lawns, painting houses, cleaning schools and parks (sweat equity). Pay it forward projects touched all kinds of demographics from lower income people at the laundromat (we paid for everyone's laundry) to business people at Starbucks by purchasing everyone's coffee. Our appreciation lunches fed every teacher, fire fighter, police officer and clinic worker in our community.

The response for Love Our City blew us away as the first year we didn't have 500 people volunteer. We had 600 show up! Because of the extra people we had to create more projects and ended up completing 70. We gave a special offering that year and the $26,000 budget was completely taken care of by the generosity of our church. It was all directly poured back into our neighborhood. In 2018 we dreamed a little bigger and it once again surprised us. We had over 1,000 people volunteer and complete 107 projects. In 2019 we grew again to 1,500 people completing 152 projects. As I am writing this we are praying for 2,000 people to do 200 projects and touch 20,000 people on the next "Love Our

City" week. This movement has become contagious. We now have businesses, corporations and donors that partner with us to sponsor and continue to make it larger. Everyone that serves gets a free Love Our City T-Shirt with the sponsors on the back. These shirts are seen all over the city as the momentum builds. Our church members invite their friends, neighbors and co-workers to come and volunteer with them on projects. It has become a signature event for the Uptown District of Tampa.

Everyone that gets touched during the week gets an invite card to the big Love Our City party at the end of the week. Guess where the party is? It's at church on Sunday! You know Crossover knows how to throw a party. We celebrate everything God did that week as we show a highlight video, have special music and we honor all the people that served. Hundreds of first time guests attend each year. We share the Gospel of Jesus in a clear, creative and compelling way. We have seen hundreds of people start a relationship with Christ on those Sundays. We followed up with them and hundreds of them got baptized the following Sunday. Many of them have become members of our church family and they now generously give back to the community.

There are hundreds of church leaders and churches that follow our church online. As people watched us post pictures and videos from Love Our City, we began getting lots of requests to help them start it in their communities. In the fall of 2018 we released a Box Leader's Kit that gives churches all the nuts and bolts on how to create Love Our City in their own neighborhoods. (www.loveourcitybook.com) It's been exciting to watch the movement grow to hundreds and hundreds of churches that are now loving their cities in new and creative ways. This all birthed from the generosity of the people at Crossover Church.

> *"What happens when you are generous?*
> *Movements are birthed!"*

*view some Love Our City photos on the next page

LOVE OUR CITY

56 • What happens when you're Generous?

Steps for success.

Meeting tangible needs and giving things away are important and necessary, but we can't stop there. We don't just want to give a hand out, we want to give a hand up. If you give a man a fish, you change his meal. If you teach a man to fish, you change his whole deal! The first few years our church was killing it with outreaches, but we needed to get better at next steps to help people develop and help people get out of poverty. I had met some pastors from Denver that had recently started this program in their church to help low income people become self-sustainable. They suggested we start a separate non-profit organization and go out and fundraise for it. Sounded like a great idea, but I told them I didn't have the time and there was nobody on our team that had the capacity either. Everyone on our small staff already was wearing multiple hats. The pastor asked if we had anyone we could partner with. I shared that we had started doing a few things with our local community development corporation. He encouraged me to meet with them and get them to do the program and raise the money and we could be a host site. Then they could give us some of the money to run the program at our location. Sounded like a great idea, but I wasn't born yesterday. It doesn't work like that. They had their own programs and they were busy doing lots of stuff already.

I went home and prayed about it and felt God telling me to at least have the conversation. So, I was obedient and invited the CEO of the Community Development Corporation to lunch. We had only known each other a little over a year and we were cool, but I never expected his response. He had brought this brochure with him about all of their new programs he wanted to tell me about. When I pitched this idea of this sustainability program he lit up and raised his voice and said, "Tommy, this is it! This is the final program I've been trying to figure out that would be the centerpiece of our new organization chart." He pointed to the graphic on the front of his folder an it had several circles coming out from a bullseye. He pointed and he said, "This program will be the middle circle, we've been trying to put our finger on it." He shared he would write up the program, raise the money and we would be a host site and they would share the funding. It was a God moment. I sat there shocked.

> *"You may not have always the resources or the time, but if it's God's plan he will make the connections and bring the provision."*

It all may start with an idea, a dream or a conversation. If God is leading you to do something to change your community, don't talk yourself out of it. Believe and push forward. A month later we went to lunch again and this time he had a full brochure of the program which he named "Steps For Success". He had several upcoming meetings with foundations to raise money for it. Within six months he raised some money and the program got launched. Our location at the church started with one part-time staff member working with five families in crisis. It was perfect as we hired a single mom from within our church that was already working with families. We wrapped it around with another part-time position from the church so we were able to have her there full-time. All five families we worked with were actually from our church. The program was customized to each family to help them level up in whatever areas they needed. Some of them needed to finish their high school diploma. Others needed to find a better job or better housing. Some of them needed a career path with a trade or college. Others had tutoring needs for their children or needed in depth marriage counseling. Most of them needed financial training as they learned how to make a budget and stick to it. We had the freedom to infuse our faith into the entire process and help these families with practical life skills. Most people in lower-income environments have very little relational capital. They don't know anyone that can help them rise up to the next level. Most of the people they know are broke and broken. This program allowed them to be around people to teach them, mentor them and help them become self-sustainable. Several people in the church became mentors to these families and we connected them with dozens of different resource partners in our community.

The Steps For Success program continued to grow over the next few years to where we had 2 full-time staff members and a part-time staff member working with close to 50 families at our site. It got so large that we ran out of families that qualified from our church, so we recruited several families from our community that needed the program. There are so many incredible stories that have come from Steps for Success. Anthony and Jackie didn't have HS diplomas. They were homeless and without sufficient income they were relying on government assistance. Through the program, they both completed their GED/HS diploma programs, were able to gain higher paying jobs, stabilized a home, learned lessons in budgeting and are no longer on government assistance! Today, they are financially stable, having added another baby to the family, growing spiritually and connected to ministry. Their next major goal is to buy their first home.

Another family had legal issues as the father was on parole for possession of an armed weapon. He had a large amount court fees to pay off and child support that he had to catch up on. They set their goals, created a vision board as a family and posted it in their living room. Within six months he had paid off his court fees, got his drivers license back and found a good paying job with FedEx. Through the program, they had a small family wedding and even enjoyed a weekend honeymoon. Their family goal was to put their children in sporting activities as they saved and followed their budgeting plans. To celebrate reaching their goals, the family went to the beach for the very first time.

Carmen was a single mom, who came from Puerto Rico with her son who was sick and in the hospital often. She found herself unable to work and eventually on section 8 with no additional income outside of her food stamps. As her son grew healthier he was able to go to Kindergarten during the day. Carmen was determined to get back on her feet for her and her son. She no longer wanted to rely on government assistance. She started in the program by walking to the church at least 2-3 times per week to study her English. As she gained confidence in her language skills, she knew she wanted to care for the sick and her goal was to go to school for nursing assistant. Through the support of Steps for Success, she was able to get her drivers' license (in English), complete school (also in English) and receive her Nursing Assistant degree. Carmen found work right away, saved to buy a car and has been working on her next goal of buying her first home.

Although the program had a site hosted at our church, we were not the ones in charge of the funding. The local Community Development Corporation went through some funding issues and decided to bring all of their external programs back under their roof at the end of 2018. Crossover no longer is a site hosting the program, but we are still connected and refer families from our church to it regularly. It is still thriving and we're grateful it is a resource changing the lives of families in our community.

Uptown mural festival.

I grew up in Philly and starting doing graffiti when I was in elementary school and was out doing illegal tagging by the time I was in high school. God got a hold of my life and since then I have used my graffiti gifts on several legal church walls and even started a clothing line that has my tag style writing on several pieces (www.eternal.clothing). I've always been an advocate for artists that are much more talented than I am. If you've been to Crossover Church you'll see several murals around our building (inside and out). Artists from all over have traveled to paint at our Flavor Fest conference. The world renowned Gospel Graffiti crew and Krosswerdz (from Australia) have done some amazing art in our kids wing, lobby and on the back outside wall of our facility.

Murals have become very popular in the past few decades in urban areas. They have beautified neighborhoods and helped several communities develop a sense of pride. These designated areas in many cities have become an attraction for artists, fans, tourists and new development. The neighborhood around our church is in transition and has several older buildings that need some love. I got together with my friend Tim Moore that started the Tampa Foundation. His foundation identifies ugly walls in our city that have a lot of eyes see them daily. He then contacts the owner and asks permission to come and beautify their property for free. If they say yes, his foundation then fundraises with donors and identifies local artists that they will hire to paint an inspiring mural. His foundation has partnered with some incredible artists that have done some great work around our city.

I pitched the idea to Tim to do a mural festival in our part of the city to make it look better and create a sense of place. He loved it and jumped into action with creating a planning team. At our first meeting I presented the idea of having the central place for the festival to be at the abandoned Flea Market next door to our church building. I have a great relationship with the owner of the property and I thought he might be on board. Everyone agreed that would be a good location. Tim and I met with the owner a few weeks later and he was super generous to give us a big yes. As I am writing this we are in our final phases of planning the first Uptown Mural Festival for the spring of 2020. A friend from California that runs Gospel Graffiti is going to curate the event as he'll recruit local and national artists to come and paint together on this 500+ foot wall. We're going to have some music, vendors and food trucks. The lasting impact will be the transformation of an eyesore in our community that will now be a cool place where people go to take pictures and admire art.

> *"These kind of changes happen in communities when generous people band together and share ideas, relationships, resources and collaborate together."*

Sidewalk kidz church.

If you want to really change a community you have to focus on the next generation. We are big on offering programs within our church for children and teens. We have an entire wing of the building dedicated to them. We also currently have two full-time staff positions that focus solely on these age groups. But, we also want to be a blessing to the children and teens outside of our church. Our annual Back 2 School Jam, Trunk or Treat and Christmas events are touch points, but we have several weekly outreaches like Sidewalk Kidz Church and Da Crew. We know many of the children and teens in our community may never step foot inside of our church building, so we go to them.

In 1995 I was a college student that came to visit Crossover Church to meet the pastor and see if I would be a good fit to come be their very first youth pastor. My interview happened while we were doing a kids program in the middle of the housing projects. I rapped a few songs on this make shift stage with a portable sound system in the Riverview Terrace Housing projects aka R.V.T. (It has since been rebuilt and is now The Oaks at Riverview.) I loved it. I knew in my heart this is where I was supposed to be. That housing project is where the youth ministry was birthed out of. Several of our members today are some of my original youth from those projects. We continued to do Sidewalk Kidz Church there until it was eventually torn down.

For years we wanted to relaunch the program, but we were waiting for the right leader, the right timing and the right place. In the first chapter I talked about recording my first album and how two generous guys helped me independently produce it. Well, both of those guys were deeply involved in Sidewalk Kidz Church with their church in St. Pete (also called Sidewalk Sunday School). They loved it so much in fact that they both moved to New York City to work at Metro Ministries with Pastor Bill Wilson. He is the guy that invented this sidewalk style kids church. He is an urban ministry legend. Eventually Marty moved back to Florida after living in Brooklyn and doing kids ministry full-time for 12 years. He soon got married and after a few years started attending Crossover. Marty got involved in the Crossover kids ministry and started regularly using his skills of illusions in his lessons. He quickly gained the nickname "Magic Marty".

In 2016 our church generously gave towards getting an outreach trailer. The trailer would be used for multiple things, but especially to relaunch Sidewalk Kidz church in Copeland Park which is right next to Shaw Elementary. Our church has a great relationship with Shaw. We have done mentoring there, the great American Teach-In and several appreciation breakfasts and lunches for teachers. We have also built a great relationship with the Parks Department as we do Sidewalk Kidz Church every Friday afternoon in Copeland Park. Every Friday Magic Marty and a team gather 40-80 neighborhood children to do a one hour program for them with music, games, fun, candy and a lesson about Jesus. The team regularly visits children and their families throughout the week. Dozens of these kids have since attended church and events at Crossover.

Sidewalk Kidz Church

Da crew.

When I was in college I was part of a ministry that went to the Juvenile Detention Centers to minister to teens that got in trouble. I had a passion for these kids. Most of them were fatherless and many of them had no real support or love. They came from rough backgrounds and needed to know about the love of Christ. I started a rap group at my college. We soon had the opportunity to go into the JDC and do a few songs and share our testimonies. It was the most engaged we ever saw the kids. I realized what a powerful tool Hip-Hop music was to reach these teens. When I came to Tampa I was invited to go into the JDC's to do music and minister. The response was incredible from both the teens and the officers. This soon led to Crossover Church starting its own weekly Juvenile Detention Center ministry. Being that I'm a Hip-Hop artist, our church has always attracted a lot of artists. The JDC ministry became a great outreach arm of our church. It created a platform for our artists to go and share their music and their stories and impact teens in our community that have been forgotten.

We have touched countless teens over the years. We're planting seeds. Many of them we never see again, but we regularly have some of them come to church after they get released. In 2004 a few rappers from our church went to the JDC and did some songs. They shared how the Gospel had changed their lives. They prayed with several young men to start a relationship with Christ. One of those teens was 17 year old Francisco Diaz. A few days later he was released and he came to Crossover Church. Some men from the church took Francisco under their wing and started to mentor him. When he turned 18 he studied really hard and completed his general contractors license. He started his own company "Heaven Sent Construction." In 2010 our church was in the process of rebuilding the former Toys R' Us store into our church. The contractor we had hired was shady. We had to fire him and find a new one. Our church leadership decided to take a chance on a young man from within our church. Francisco was 23 years old by this time and had grown his company to 16 full-time employees. Although he was young, he was smart, organized and ambitious. He was God's man for the job. He took on the 43,000 square foot construction project and absolutely crushed it! He rebid the project and saved the church close to $700,000. At the end of the project we ran out of money and he offered to loan us the money to finish it. I told him that was generous, but we needed $200,000. He told me that was exactly what his company had in the bank. All this time he had been saving up money for his company. At that moment he realized that he had been saving it up to loan it to his church to help us finish the project. Who would have ever guessed that just six years before we were ministering to him as a teenager from the hood in JDC? He saved us $700k and loaned us $200k and built our new church in record time! Wow! Look at God!

You never know who you are ministering to.

> *"There are so many hurting people in our communities and in our prisons that have a call of God on their lives with incredible potential and purpose."*

God uses generous people to give their time, talent and treasure to impact them and help them level up. Our JDC ministry is still going strong and today is known as "Da Crew". We have a team that goes in weekly to do a Bible Study, music, concerts and events. The department of juvenile corrections loves our church as the teens and officers deeply connect with our team. Several of our team members have rough backgrounds that the kids can really relate to. While other team members may not share the same history, they are still able to connect due to their genuine hearts. Our church donates backpacks, school supplies and hygiene kits to these teens throughout the year. We're able to bless them with free Bibles and devotional books from our church. Da Crew also hosts a Christmas party and several other events throughout the year where we feed these kids and let them know they are loved. All of this is possible because of the generosity of our church family. There are so many success stories of teens that have turned their lives around.

Our "Da Crew" leadership team under Frank Jones is dreaming about purchasing a home in our neighborhood for older teen boys that are transitioning into adulthood and have no family support. Without a way out, many of these young men will likely become another statistic and end up in adult prison. The program in this home will include mentoring, character development, community involvement, education and fitness. Our church will be the base for spiritual development. It is exciting to watch leaders from within rise up and have generous visions for their community. We can't wait to see what God does next.

G3.

"When generosity gets into the DNA of your church, you'll begin to see God give visions to individuals and families to meet needs in your community."

We have created an environment for this at our church. I am a kingdom entrepreneur. My mind is always turning to create new ways to help other leaders win, reach more people and creatively develop new streams of funding to help us accomplish the vision. They say you attract people like you. Crossover Church has a growing base of entrepreneurs and business owners, but I'm especially excited about the non-profit entrepreneurs rising up. They are starting their own non-profit organizations to meet needs in the community that they are passionate about. One of these incredible organizations from our church family is G3.

G3 stands for Give God Glory! It was a vision that Joshua Balloon had back in 2007 while he was in college. He dreamt of starting a mentoring program that gave at risk kids the knowledge, experiences, love and opportunities that he had been given as a youth. Josh grew up in the city, but had a solid Godly home with both parents fully engaged. He and his cousin Ronnie starting visiting kids in hospitals and also launched several football camps for high schools in need. That soon developed into a sports program that met every Sunday afternoon. They started with prayer, followed by training, exercising and then feeding everyone some healthy snacks. It kicked off with just seven kids and quickly exploded to over one hundred coming every Sunday. They called it church on the field. Sports was the initial draw, but they soon added more mental and spiritual applications and turned it into a full blown mentoring program. Their most popular initiative is the "Be More Program". It focuses on finishing strong, following up and following through. They creatively incentivize the program and reward them along the way for their hard work. This includes a big banquet in the summer where most of the kids walk out with gifts as if it were Christmas.

Since their inception in 2013 they have reached over 5,000 youth. They currently work with over 400 youth through all of their programs that include, The Literacy Program, Stem Program, College Bound, Leaders in Transition, Recreational Therapy, Athletic Program, Tutoring Program and the Be More program. G3 has over 30 committed volunteers that pour into the next generation. They get their annual budget through services that they outsource to various schools, churches, parks and community centers year round. In addition they have several donors, sponsors and fundraisers. Their goal is to eventually start a sustainable academy where they can impact the youth that they serve on a greater scale within a school setting. Their dream is to expand G3 to other cities impacting as many youth as possible; mentally, spiritually and physically as they give God all the glory.

Economic empowerment.

Our culture is rapidly changing. There is disruption happening in every industry. Amazon has changed the way we shop. Uber has changed the way we catch a ride and Netflix and Spotify have changed the way we consume movies, shows and music. New jobs will be created as technology continues to advance and other jobs will disappear. There are more and more people starting their own businesses, doing contract work or side hustles. The gig economy is exploding. CNBC.com estimates that the majority of workers in the U.S. will become contract workers by 2027.

> *"If people are not economically empowered about this coming change they will get left behind."*

We already see a growing gap between the wealthy and the poor and this is expected to increase in the years to come. Our church has offered several classes and small groups for entrepreneurs and business owners to help them use Biblical principles as they network and level up.

In the 2020's Crossover Church will focus on this area more than ever as the need is quickly growing. We are launching an entrepreneurship course that will be hosted in our new coffee shop. New partnerships are forming for us to be able to host shark tank style events to help new businesses gain capital, relationships and partnerships to help them scale up. As our neighborhood and city grows and redevelops, our desire is that everyone has opportunities to rise with the tide and not drown. Our focus is not just on creating wealth for people, but teaching them to give back and be generous with their wealth so it can change lives and have an eternal impact for God's purposes.

Watch "Your Community Changes" @
www.youtube.com/urband813

Community Changes:

1. What is a Love Our City story that you have been a part of?

2. What are some major needs in our community?
   How can you help tackle them?

3. What are some ideas that God has put on your heart to help change your community?

4. What story of community change in this chapter got you most excited?

5. How do you think your community will change in the next 10 years?
   How can your church get ready for these changes?

EPILOGUE

The topic of giving is complicated and opinions on how we should give can vary widely. Giving is a deeply personal thing between the giver and God. We as believers know we should give generously to God's work, but how much, when and to whom are always extremely difficult to determine. We are inundated with choices and options as there are countless great ministries and causes competing for our discretionary resources. Over decades of giving, my wife and I have developed a process that at least works for us. It may be helpful to you especially if you are new to the giving process.

The first and most important step we take in our process is to commit the decision to prayer followed by asking the following questions; Where is the Holy Spirit directing us? What ministries has God connected us with over time? What are we passionate about? We then perform our due diligence on the small group of ministries we have identified.

1.) Who leads the ministry? What do we know about this person? Do they have integrity? What are their true motives? What is their track record and history?

2.) What is the leader's long-term vision? Can they clearly articulate their vision and mission and does it align with our passion?

3.) Have they developed a good team to help them accomplish their goals? This is critical for success. They should be able to share specifics about the team structure.

4.) Is their mission truly Biblical? Will it truly impact people and expand God's kingdom? This should be a given, but unfortunately it's not always the case.

5.) Are the leaders hard working? This should also be a given, but we unfortunately have found that some ministries have a sense of entitlement and therefore feel little need to deliver the effort and work that is needed to accomplish their mission.

6.) What are the results? The ministry should be able to demonstrate some quantifiable results and demonstrate growth and sustainability.

Although this may seem like a strict process, we feel it is our duty as stewards of God's financial resources to choose those ministries that can truly impact the world. One such ministry we have found that meets all these criteria plus more is Crossover Church. Through Pastor Tommy's vision, hard work and strong stable leadership, Crossover has reached thousands for the Kingdom and the future is bright. We have partnered with Crossover for over a decade and we can't express the deep joy we receive giving to this ministry.

Although contrary to some popular preaching, the act of giving may not result in the giver being blessed with big financial resources. However, what the giver will always be blessed with is true joy, and an opportunity to impact God's kingdom for eternity! We are certain that our investment in Crossover Church will produce an enormous return for eternity that can never fall in value or be erased.

- Dave and Bonnie - Naples, Fl

ABOUT CROSSOVER CHURCH

Crossover was started in the early 90's to reach people in the urban community that weren't going to the traditional church. In 1996 Pastor Joe McCutchen brought in Tommy Kyllonen to start the youth ministry. Over the next six years a new model of urban youth ministry was birthed that reached hundreds of unchurched teens and young adults. In 2002 the church was relaunched with new vision and structure as Tommy became the lead pastor. Crossover carefully and prayerfully began to make several changes to better reach the community. The service grew quickly as several new people came and built relationships with Christ and get discipled.

God has called Crossover to be a pioneering church in reaching those influenced by Urban/Hip-Hop Culture. Crossover is not a "Hip-Hop Church", they are a New Testament Church in the 21st century in the urban context. So, you will find Hip-Hop as well as R and B, Gospel, EDM, Reggae, Spanish music and many different rhythmic styles in their worship services. Because of the church's unique approach they have been featured in USA Today, Newsweek, CBS News, BET News and several local media outlets. Outreach Magazine listed them as one of America's Most Innovative Churches. As many around the world began to look at Crossover as a model they launched the Flavor Fest Urban Leadership Conference. 5,000 leaders have been trained at the conference over the years. Numerous CD's, books, magazines and resources have been produced by Pastor Tommy and other innovators at the church.

Their former North Orleans campus was completely renovated and transformed into a place exploding with creativity. At that location the church grew from 40 to close to 500 that attended 3 Sunday Services. Although the North Orleans campus was a cool space, it was maxed out. Pastor Tommy and the leadership team prayed about the next steps and even in the middle of a recession they along with the membership decided to put the campus up for sale in late 2008. In January of 2010 the campus was sold to another church and Crossover became a portable church meeting at a hotel. They experienced a season of more growth and miracles at the hotel. During this time they signed a deal on a former Toys R' Us retail building. In the Fall of 2010 they moved into their newly remodeled 43,000 square foot facility on Fowler Ave. Since then they have been able to reach the city in multiple new ways as they have seen thousands start a new relationship with Christ and over 1,500 people get baptized. In 2019 they nationally launched their Love Our City campaign to equip churches to reach thousands of new people in their communities. Hundreds of churches have joined the growing Love Our City movement. The church also launched their new location in the city of Atlanta in 2019 - Crossover Church ATL! This was all possible because of the generosity of the people of God!

Sunday Worship Experience @ Crossover

CROSSOVER CHURCH
DISCOVER · DEVELOP · DISPLAY

www.crossoverchurch.org

follow us on all social platforms "Crossover813"

NEW BOOK + CD FROM
TOMMY "URBAN D." KYLLONEN

30 DAY DEVOTIONAL BOOK, VIDEO SERIES, CD AND A MOVEMENT THAT CAN CHANGE YOUR LIFE, YOUR CHURCH AND YOUR CITY!

AVAILABLE AT

amazon · **audible** · **kindle**
MUSIC · **iTunes** · **Spotify**

AND

WWW.LOVEOURCITYBOOK.COM

EVERYTHING YOUR CHURCH OR ORGANIZATION NEEDS TO REACH THOUSANDS OF NEW PEOPLE IN YOUR COMMUNITY!

JOIN HUNDREDS OF CHURCHES IN THE LOVE OUR CITY MOVEMENT AS THE LEADERS KIT INCLUDES A THUMB DRIVE WITH A MESSAGE SERIES, SMALL GROUP VIDEO CURRICULUM, ARTWORK, VIDEOS, PROJECT TEMPLATES, THE NEW LOVE OUR CITY HIP-HOP CD AND MORE. PLUS, THE LEADERS GUIDE GIVES YOU THE NUTS AND BOLTS ON HOW TO GET CORPORATE SPONSORS AND RAISE UP AN ARMY OF VOLUNTEERS TO SERVE THOUSANDS.

AVAILABLE EXCLUSIVELY AT
WWW.LOVEOURCITYBOOK.com

"ETERNAL"

clothing

www.eternal.clothing @eternalclothingline

About the author.

Tommy "Urban D." Kyllonen has been in ministry for over 20 years at Crossover Church in Tampa, Florida. He has been the lead pastor for over 15 years. Under his leadership the church has seen incredible growth. This multi-ethnic, multi-generational, multi-class church has become a model. As they grew, they relocated into a 43,000-square foot retail building that was a former Toys R' Us in Tampa's Uptown District. Outreach Magazine recognized Crossover as one of America's Most Innovative Churches. Crossover has also been featured in USA Today, Newsweek, CBS News, BET News, and several regional media outlets. Urban D. is an internationally known hip-hop artist who has released 9 full-length albums and several remix projects. (**www.urband.org**).

Tommy has authored 5 books. His most acclaimed book "Love Our City" is a 30-day devotional format for churches and small groups to go through together. It also includes a community service project aspect. His church has used this to reach thousands of new people. They created a leaders box kit that gives churches all the tools to launch Love Our City. There are hundreds of churches that have joined the Love Our City Movement. Tommy is also the publisher of S.O.U.LMAG Magazine, which has produced 28 issues. Tommy has a passion to help other leaders win. He founded the Flavor Fest Urban Leadership Conference, which has trained over 5,000 leaders. His coaching network has trained over 100 urban pastors and church planters. He serves as the vice-chair of the Uptown Tampa Innovation Partnership board. He lives in Tampa, Florida with his wife Lucy and his two daughters Deyana and Sophia.